T0210118

Forgive Anyway

A 30-day writing journey to total forgiveness

SHERYL WALKER

authorHOUSE®

AuthorHouse™
1663 Liberty Drive
Bloomington, IN 47403
www.authorhouse.com
Phone: 1 (800) 839-8640

Published by AuthorHouse 02/06/2020

ISBN: 978-1-7283-4563-5 (sc)
ISBN: 978-1-7283-4562-8 (e)

Library of Congress Control Number: 2020902012

Print information available on the last page.

Forgiveness is an intentional decision to release negative feelings of anger, resentment, or vengeance toward a person or group who has inflicted harm, regardless of whether or not they "deserve" to be forgiven. It is a change that happens within the heart and mind of the person that was wronged.

Forgiveness means "I will not relate to you based on what you did."

"There's nothing done or said that can't be forgiven." – Matthew 12: 31-32 (MSG)

"Father forgive them for they know not what they do." – Luke 23: 24 (ESV)

We are most like God when we forgive.

Forgiveness is medicine for the soul.

Despite it all, forgive anyway.

INTRODUCTION

In reflecting on the patterns in my life, I have found forgiveness to be one of the most beneficial decisions we can make to improve the quality of our lives. It is also one of the greatest challenges in action. This "unsolvable" problem has such power. It keeps people stuck in anger and remorse. It has the capacity to keep some people's entire lives completely frozen. How could the antagonist have so much power? We could easily spend a lifetime wondering, *How could they have said that? How could they have done that?* This led me to become more and more intrigued by the notion of forgiveness. I had personally wasted too much time repeating offenses in my mind, while remaining frozen in disbelief and feelings of anger. Anger wasn't serving me. Neither was retelling the same story. How could I bridge the gap between the anger and pain I was feeling now, and the place of peace, understanding, and love I wanted to get to? How could I stop these feelings from controlling my life? Was it even possible? Without forgiveness, families and communities would never survive. Anger, when held on to, completely destroys all our relationships: family structure, social networks, professional communities, and more.

Life is unsustainable without forgiveness. It is our lifeline. Our hearts would never be healed without it. There are a few things I have found to be true about anger and forgiveness from my own experience:

- The answer can't be to end every relationship where deep hurt has occurred. Eventually, this would eliminate all meaningful relationships.
- My antagonist often felt deep remorse, and was often also wrestling with their own issues. Many of the hurts I received

seemed to be accidents or mistakes, but they still left semi-permanent walls.

- Relationships can deepen and grow stronger if we can work through the pain and anger.
- I can forgive certain people more quickly and more easily than others, like my young child, where "unconditional love" is present.
- When there was a label or expectation (e.g. parent, spouse, sibling), and the person fell short, the anger and bitterness was even greater. There was also more of a desire for vengeance and feelings of superiority. They were wrong and I was right.
- When a solid relationship had not yet been formed, it was easy to cut a person off and no longer invest in the relationship. A few strikes and they were out.
- Not all relationships were meant to last forever. Some were in fact seasonal and intended to teach us specific lessons.
- It was harder to forgive when the antagonist's weakness was my strength.
- I was more forgiving when I had done the same thing that someone was now doing to me. I had in fact walked a mile in their shoes. I had much more empathy.

The Bible repeatedly states things such as:

- Forgive like Christ has forgiven you (Colossians 3: 13) (Ephesians 4: 32)
- If I don't forgive, God will not forgive me (Matthew 6: 14-15)
- Christ died on the cross for our sins. I don't need to continue to crucify others for their offenses (Ephesians 1: 7)
- If someone sins against me repeatedly, I must continue to forgive them (Luke 17: 3-4)
- Do not judge other people – their words and actions (Matthew 7: 1-6)
- Love your enemies. Be kind to those that hate you (Matthew 5: 44)
- Anger is a natural response in certain situations. I cannot allow it to turn to sin (Ephesians 4: 26)

- Put away bitterness and anger (Ephesians 4: 31)
- Make amends and allowances for sins committed against you (Isaiah 1: 18)

The Research & Process

So, began my exploration. I reflected on every relationship, past and present. I read a few books, watched videos and documentaries, and talked to people.

The Structure

When I thought of a structure or format that helped me heal in the past, I recalled a 30-day writing challenge I had participated in a few years prior, during a time I was broken and confused at the cards life had dealt me. In retrospect, those cards were a true blessing. The writing journey served as a healing ritual and lifted me out of a dark place. This led me to reflect on how I could rewrite my current painful 'failed attempt at forgiveness' story into a story of transformation and victory.

The Outcome

Going through each day, one by one, moved me along the forgiveness continuum. I am currently not an expert forgiver by any means, but I do interpret offenses differently. I try to carve out reflection time, when I sense I am becoming angry or holding on to a grudge. I aim to control only that which I can, which is feeling good right now.

The Bottom Line

The scripture says, "**For we wrestle not against flesh and blood, but against principalities, against powers, against the rulers of the darkness of this world, against spiritual wickedness in high**

places" -Ephesians 6: 12 (KJV). Forgiveness is a weapon for spiritual warfare. The enemy uses the offenses from our antagonist(s) to fill our minds with negative thoughts about that person and about ourselves. The enemy is not the antagonist. The enemy is the principality operating within the antagonist. The enemy is beyond what the eyes can see and is working through another to cause various hurts, conflict, and disruptions. The enemy accesses this person through the various traumas and wounds this person is carrying around. Once we realize we are not fighting a person, we can more easily extend grace, mercy, and forgiveness. Refuse to assist the devil by harboring unforgiveness.

Get Ready

In the subsequent pages, you will be presented with a daily forgiveness passage. These pages will guide you to think about what you should write each day. Pour your heart out onto the pages that have been provided. Read, reflect, write, and heal.

I hope that you will benefit from this 30-day journey and make the choice to forgive. You deserve to live a full life, free from the bondage of anger and pain.[1]

---

[1] Note: This 30-day forgiveness journey is not a replacement for therapy or counseling services. Please consult your doctor.

So, chosen by God for this new life of love, dress in the wardrobe God picked out for you: compassion, kindness, humility, quiet strength, discipline. Be even-tempered, content with second place, quick to forgive an offense. **Forgive as quickly and completely as the Master forgave you.** And regardless of what else you put on, wear love. It's your basic, all-purpose garment. Never be without it.

— Colossians 3: 12-14 (MSG)

DAY 1

A Day for Prayer

Prayer

Lord, I have a confession in my heart:
I am struggling to forgive.
Soften my heart Lord. Give me the courage
To love others better.
I know your son died so that I might be forgiven.
You grant me endless grace and endless mercy.
You see my heart and not my faults.
You love me despite of me.
Lord teach me how to be more like you.
Show me how to love through my heartache.
I surrender it all to you.
I am harboring resentment.
Heal me God. Hold me in your arms.
Show me how to let it go, once and for all.
Show me that there is a way out of the bondage.
Show me the path to freedom and love.
Bring the joy and happiness back to my life.
Grant me compassion and understanding.
No one is sinless. We are all imperfect.
Mistakes happen.
Lord, wipe away my tears.

No matter what I do or is done to me,
Please allow me to remain loving.
Show me how to forgive completely.
Rid me of all bitterness, resentment, and a desire for revenge.
Allow me to let it go and proceed forward in love.
Remembering nothing is personal.
Please Lord heal me.
Mend my brokenness as a result of this situation.
Make me whole again.
Bless the antagonist God.
Grant them healing.
Grant us both a renewed heart and mind.
Antagonist, I forgive you and I also forgive myself.
Let us be both be abundantly blessed and whole again.
Amen

Pray without ceasing. Pray that God softens your heart and opens your mind to the path of complete forgiveness. We must also pray for our enemies. God will bring a revelation to our enemies.

Day 1 Prompt: Write your own forgiveness prayer on the lines below.

"In prayer there is a connection between what God does and what you do. **You can't get forgiveness from God, for instance, without also forgiving others.** If you refuse to do your part, you cut yourself off from God's part."

— Matthew 6: 14-15 (MSG)

DAY 2

A Day to Reflect on God's Grace and Mercy

How God Forgives

How does God forgive us? God forgives us totally and completely. This is how we can aim to forgive others and ourselves. His love covers a multitude of sins. He holds no grudges and doesn't keep a list of all of our wrongdoings. He gets no satisfaction when we feel overburdened with guilt. He never gives up on us. God knows our dark side and every sin we have committed, yet he forgives, and loves us unconditionally. He does not air out our dirty laundry. What would Jesus do in some of the situations we find ourselves in where we harbor unforgiveness? He accepts us with all of our imperfections. While we will never be God, we can try to move along the continuum and get closer to His ways. It is natural to get stuck in negative emotions, but now might be the time to begin to get unstuck. You have probably been legitimately mistreated and have a reason to feel badly. You may have been betrayed and deeply hurt. Forgiveness does not excuse the indignities. God tells us that despite these realities, we should obey his commands and forgive: release the anger, the desire for vengeance, and the judgment we inflict. Approach the forgiveness journey with humility. We are imperfect beings learning and growing along life's journey. We are the hardest on ourselves, but if God can forgive us, we should forgive ourselves also.

Day 2 Prompt: Reflect on this notion of complete forgiveness. Bridge the gap between where you are now and the goal of total forgiveness. What are you holding on to that you need to release? How will you reprogram your thoughts about the person in question? Where would we be if God held onto our offenses and did not show us grace and mercy? Who are the primary people you need to forgive, and what it is you need to forgive them for? What would Jesus do?

_____

_____

_____

_____

_____

_____

_____

_____

_____

_____

_____

_____

_____

_____

_____

_____

_____

_____

_____

_____

"If we claim that we're free of sin, we're only fooling ourselves. A claim like that is errant nonsense. On the other hand, if we admit our sins—make a clean breast of them—he won't let us down; he'll be true to himself. **He'll forgive our sins and purge us of all wrongdoing.** If we claim that we've never sinned, we out-and-out contradict God—make a liar out of him. A claim like that only shows off our ignorance of God."

— 1 John 1: 8-10 (MSG)

DAY 3

A Day to Forgive Yourself

Self-Forgiveness I

We all need forgiveness. When we hurt someone, we long to be forgiven. We are only human, and bound to make mistakes. We forget imperfection is part of the human experience. No one was intended to be perfect. Cut yourself some slack.

Forgive yourself for saying or doing what you thought was right at the time but taken the wrong way.

Forgive yourself for the mistakes of your past that impact your present.

Forgive yourself for not seeing the red flags soon enough and staying in a situation too long. Forgive yourself for believing the judgments people concluded about you, or the false story about yourself that stems from childhood wounds.

Forgive yourself for disappointing others even though it was the best you could do in the moment.

Forgive yourself for being so stuck in unforgiveness that it has crippled you in many ways. Forgive yourself for the naivety of your youth. You are older and wiser now. You are not the same person you were then.

Forgive yourself for holding on to guilt, regret, shame, or remorse. We tend to beat ourselves up when we believe we have missed the mark in certain areas of our life.

Forgive yourself for betraying yourself, your family, or not being as supportive as you could have been.

Day 3 Prompt: Where do you need to extend grace and mercy to yourself? Did your mistake impact others you love? In what ways could you show yourself extra love care and compassion? What negative beliefs about yourself do you need to release? How could you change your personal narrative and lift yourself out of this negative self-concept? How can you rewrite the script and see the best in yourself? You are a child of the most High. He uses our imperfections to carry out his work and glorify his name. If he forgives you, aim to forgive yourself.

"Summing up: **Be agreeable, be sympathetic, be loving, be compassionate, be humble**. That goes for all of you, no exceptions. No retaliation. No sharp-tongued sarcasm. Instead, **bless—that's your job: to bless. You'll be a blessing and also get a blessing.**

Whoever wants to embrace life
　　and see the day fill up with good,
Here's what you do:
　　Say nothing evil or hurtful;
Snub evil and cultivate good;
　　run after peace for all you're worth.
God looks on all this with approval,
　　listening and responding well to what he's asked;
But he turns his back
　　on those who do evil things."

— 1 Peter 3: 8-12 (MSG)

DAY 4

A Day for Acceptance

Acceptance

Acceptance is important on the road to forgiveness. We cannot change the past or what took place, society and the historical constructs, or people and their life circumstances that have shaped them. We cannot force people to be more aware of our feelings. We must accept life as it is, people, ourselves, and the imperfections of life. We cannot expect others to be anyone but themselves. People are complicated creatures. We must leave them in God's hands. God charges us to love people, not to change people. That is His job. Accept who they are and determine how you will operate in that situation. Accept the past. Release the past. Accept all that is and all that is to come. Whatever is for you, wherever you are to be, will never be withheld from you. We are all walking around with invisible wounds. How others view situations is based on their experience. Detach from your entanglement with other people's issues and all the hopes you may have had for that relationship. Many have experienced traumas and still live from that place of brokenness. If a person demonstrates unfavorable patterns of behavior, we must accept that this is who they are and where they are on their journey. We cannot expedite their growth. Oftentimes they do not see an issue with their actions, and if they do, they may not be willing or able to make an immediate change. They might even turn the tables on us, blame us for their wrongdoing, and attempt to invalidate our feelings and perceptions. Some people are unable to see you stand in your truth. Your strength makes them feel inadequate and they lash out. They consistently act in an unfavorable manner. This is a reality you will have to accept.

Day 4 Prompt: What other realities do you need to accept? Are you wishing someone was who they are not? Or that the past could be different than it actually was? Do you wish they could see into themselves more than they do? What would it take to accept the person as they are? You don't have to accept their pain or abuse, but you have to come to grips with who they are and what they have done, and may continue to do, and decide how you will operate in that knowing. This is really all you can control. Reflect on this notion of acceptance. What will you do differently after fully accepting the antagonist and what they bring to the table?

"Jesus was matter-of-fact: 'Embrace this God-life. Really embrace it, and nothing will be too much for you. This mountain, for instance: Just say, "Go jump in the lake"—no shuffling or shilly-shallying—and it's as good as done. That's why I urge you to pray for absolutely everything, ranging from small to large. Include everything as you embrace this God-life, and you'll get God's everything. And when you assume the posture of prayer, remember that it's not all asking. **If you have anything against someone, forgive—only then will your heavenly Father be inclined to also wipe your slate clean of sins.**'"

— Mark 11: 22-25 (MSG)

DAY 5

A Day to Extend Grace and Mercy

Grace and Mercy

If we are in relationship with others, they are bound to hurt us and we will hurt them. It comes with the territory. The pain we experience from other people tends to be the worst and most frequent pain we endure in life. Have realistic expectations. Many times, the other person's intention was not to hurt us. See their humanity. How could we extend mercy to the antagonist? We could choose to have selective memory and release people from their offenses. We must do the same with ourselves. Be merciful with yourself. Sometimes the pain of hurting someone we love is such a heavy burden and it is too much for us to carry. Jesus already died on the cross for our sins; we do not have to crucify anyone in spirit or in thought. Their debts have already been paid. If we were to hurt someone deeply, wouldn't we want the same grace and mercy extended to us?

Day 5 Prompt: What does living a life with grace look like? How can we soften our heart? How can we want for ourselves what we cannot do for others? What price are we paying emotionally, financially, spiritually, for lack of forgiveness? How does this serve us? Are we going to reduce this person to one or a few poor decisions? Can we separate the person from the act and look at mercy from that perspective?

"If I give everything I own to the poor and even go to the stake to be burned as a martyr, but I don't love, I've gotten nowhere. So, no matter what I say, what I believe, and what I do, I'm bankrupt without love.

Love never gives up.
Love cares more for others than for self.
Love doesn't want what it doesn't have.
Love doesn't strut,
Doesn't have a swelled head,
Doesn't force itself on others,
Isn't always 'me first,'
Doesn't fly off the handle,
Doesn't keep score of the sins of others,
Doesn't revel when others grovel,
Takes pleasure in the flowering of truth,
Puts up with anything,
Trusts God always,
Always looks for the best,
Never looks back,
But keeps going to the end."

— 1 Corinthians 13: 5-7 (MSG)

DAY 6

A Day to Stop Personalizing Offenses

Nothing Is Personal

Take nothing personally. When hurtful events occur, we often immediately personalize the event, thinking it has something to do with us. We attach so much meaning to events that occur. Learn not to be offended. If you do great things in life, offenses will come and you must learn to brush them off immediately. We can't fight all the battles and attacks that come our way. Fight the ones that matter. The hurtful things people say and do are a reflection of themselves and not of you. They could be undergoing pressure, tired, holding on to something you said or did in the past, not taking responsibility for their own actions, and a host of other reasons that will remain unknown to you. Many of us are still processing childhood wounds and acting out from that place and space. Many times, these individuals don't even recognize that what they said or did was hurtful or offensive. Hurt people hurt people. Unhappy people want you to be unhappy too. If you internalize these actions, you will compromise your quality of life by altering your perception of yourself. When we receive the lash out or deflection of unresolved pain, this has nothing to do with us. When they make rude comments and digs at your character here and there, say to yourself, "I will not personalize the words and actions of others."

Day 6 Prompt: How does someone else's selfishness or unkind behavior dictate your joy or misery? You are still wonderful and worthy. Have you shared with them when boundaries have been crossed? Does it seem foreign to you that people who are abusive have an inner turmoil that has nothing to do with you? Maybe they have never had models of appropriate behavior or a way to process their own personal pain. Maybe their own insecurities are overwhelming them. Your gifts and talents might be too big for a place and space. Perhaps the intent was truly to never hurt you, but a result of some other pain they were experiencing. Reflect on this notion of not personalizing other people's actions.

_____

_____

_____

_____

_____

_____

_____

_____

_____

_____

_____

_____

_____

_____

_____

_____

_____

Sheryl Walker

"Make a clean break with all cutting, backbiting, profane talk. Be gentle with one another, sensitive. **Forgive one another as quickly and thoroughly as God in Christ forgave you.**"

— Ephesians 4: 31-32 (MSG)

DAY 7

A Day to Seek Understanding

Understanding

Putting yourself in someone else's shoes can give you some sense of perspective. Try to understand the hurt and pain that caused them to behave the way that they did. If we carried the same storyline, maybe we would behave in a similar manner. Is the antagonist going through a rough season in life and are overwhelmed with disappointment? People are often doing the best that they can. We all suffer through painful life experiences. The antagonist may not understand how their behavior is received. Are they themselves surrounded by abuse in some form? Are their current insecurities so loud they can't behave as their best self? Could we have misinterpreted their intent? Can you sift through the painful part and glean some understanding?

Day 7 Prompt: Can you aim today to seek understanding? Can you offer compassion to the antagonist? Could they also be wounded and suffering? Can you offer compassion and empathy to yourself? Understanding does not mean the actions were ok. Understanding provides perspective.

"God will defeat your enemies who attack you. They'll come at you on one road and run away on seven roads."

— Deuteronomy 28: 7 (MSG)

DAY 8

A Day to Give Yourself Time and Space

Time and Space

Sometimes time and space speed up the path to forgiveness and aid with the healing process. If time and time again, being in the presence of the antagonist stirs up negative emotions, avoid them for a while. When you remove yourself from the pain, wounds might begin healing. You might have a chance to deal with the loss of the relationship you thought you had. Anger might subside. You might not be triggered as frequently. It might also send a message, that boundaries are being crossed. Can you remove yourself from the antagonist temporarily or even permanently? If you must remain in the situation, how are you going to operate in the situation for your own healing and self-preservation?

Day 8 Prompt: Determine the boundaries that are necessary for you during this healing process. Reflect on this notion of time and space. In what ways do you believe this can help with forgiveness?

"If your heart is broken, you'll find God right there;
if you're kicked in the gut, he'll help you catch your breath."

— Psalm 34: 18 (MSG)

DAY 9

A Day to Stop Rehashing the Offense

Rehashing the Past Offense

Forgiveness brings peace of mind. Rehashing the offenses often replays in our mind like a broken record. It gets us wound up, assigning blame, and seeking revenge. It is truly a form of torture. It opens the door to further negative emotions and isolates us from others. LET IT GO. When we overthink, we waste precious time. Surrender your pain to God. Stop retelling the painful offenses that were inflicted on you or that you inflicted. Live in the present. Recognize the pain you suffered without letting that pain define you, enabling you to heal and move on with your life. The past is a trap that tends to keep us bound. This ability to move past the pain takes an incredible amount of strength. You will have to reframe the events that took place, release the pain, and no longer dwell on the past. We tend to blame the other person for how we feel. Blame may pacify us temporarily, but it doesn't change anything. It makes us the victim. This keeps us imprisoned and stuck in the pain. There is great freedom and liberation when we release these negative feelings. Pivot your attention and energy to someone or something that needs your attention now. Forgiveness is not about what they did, but about obeying God's command and walking in his loving power. From today on, officially retire the painful story.

Day 9 Prompt: How does dwelling on the past prevent you from forgiving? If you agree that you cannot change the past, how does dwelling on it serve you? Can you shift your thoughts to your loving relationship with God, knowing ALL is for good, even the perceived bad? What do you need to stop rehashing in your mind? How can you move forward in peace and positivity?

"Be alert. If you see your friend going wrong, correct him. **If he responds, forgive him. Even if it's personal against you and repeated seven times through the day, and seven times he says, 'I'm sorry, I won't do it again,' forgive him."**

— Luke 17: 3-4 (MSG)

DAY 10

A Day to Set Boundaries

Repeat Antagonists

Repeat antagonists need boundaries. There might have to be certain supports that are always in place during your interactions. We cannot allow ourselves to be continuously abused. We cannot continuously take the bait and fall into the traps these individuals set for us, such as engaging in arguments that lead to nowhere. We must never lower ourselves. Forgiving does not mean forgetting or denying what took place. Some people are unkind, ill, or deeply wounded and act out as a result of these wounds. Many of these antagonists insist on being in the superior position by any means necessary. As we grow and become wiser, they want to keep us fixed in a state of submission. There is often nothing we can do to change the reality of their disturbing behavior. Sometimes we can change the frequency and intensity of our interactions. You might live in constant fear that they will hurt you again. God does not give us a spirit of fear. Do not let anger or fear control you. God is a protector. Call out to Him and he will tell you how to respond. Sometimes the best response is silence and removing yourself from the environment. Other times the best response is to have a conversation or a series of conversations until something changes. A next step might be to bring in a third party. What are some boundaries you need to put in place? Again, no matter what new offenses the antagonist attacks you with, rise higher!

Day 10 Prompt: How will you protect yourself from repeat antagonists but still proceed in faith and confidence that no matter what happens, God will protect you? While repeat offenders must be forgiven each and every time, how can you forgive but at the same time protect?

_____

_____

_____

_____

_____

_____

_____

_____

_____

_____

_____

_____

_____

_____

_____

_____

_____

_____

_____

_____

_____

"**Bless your enemies; no cursing under your breath.** Laugh with your happy friends when they're happy; share tears when they're down. Get along with each other; don't be stuck-up. Make friends with nobodies; don't be the great somebody."

— Romans 12: 14-16 (MSG)

DAY 11

A Day to Release the Villain Story

Release the Villain Story

Refrain from speaking negatively about the antagonist. When we speak negatively of others, this gives them power in our lives. Even though we may feel they warrant it, villainizing someone until they become a real-life monster in our subconscious is unhealthy. We form a negative attachment to this person and the anger and resentment we feel towards them. No one is advocating for you to ignore new indignities that are inflicted. You must still go into prayer and ask God how to address those. Aim to bless others with your words. Do not curse them. We could be reflecting on God's goodness and our multitude of blessings, not on the person that has inflicted harm.

Day 11 Prompt: Do you say the name or think about the person that hurt you and continues to hurt you several times throughout the day? If so, what else could you discuss, other than that person? Or is this a message that you need to mend that connection? What we focus our attention on is drawn to us. If it is someone we have to interact with daily, how can we rewrite the script and make the villain into a new character—and most importantly, not the main character? Can we give them the grace to begin anew?

_____

_____

_____

_____

_____

_____

_____

_____

_____

_____

_____

_____

_____

_____

_____

_____

_____

_____

_____

_____

"**Keep vigilant watch over your heart;**
   that's where life starts.
Don't talk out of both sides of your mouth;
   avoid careless banter, white lies, and gossip.
Keep your eyes straight ahead;
   ignore all sideshow distractions.
Watch your step,
   and the road will stretch out smooth before you.
Look neither right nor left;
   leave evil in the dust."

— Proverbs 4: 23-27 (MSG)

DAY 12

A Day to Release the Offense

Release Ritual

Do a release ritual. Write a letter to the person or people that caused you harm and tell them how their behavior made you feel. Imagine them in your mind. Then discard that letter and wish them well in your heart. This is a symbol of letting things go. Have zero expectations of them changing or improving. Outwardly expressing how you feel can be very healing and might bring some closure that is needed. Remember, no one owes you anything, including an apology, despite the things they may have said and done, and despite the title they hold in your life (friend, family, colleague, etc.). Whenever feelings of anger resurface, just state, "I forgive you and wish you well." Count this as a new beginning.

Day 12 Prompt: Write a letter below to the person or people that caused you harm and tell them how their behavior made you feel. Imagine them in your mind. Reflect on how you felt after that release ritual.

_____

_____

_____

_____

_____

_____

_____

_____

_____

_____

_____

_____

_____

_____

_____

_____

_____

_____

_____

_____

"This is God's Word on the subject: 'As soon as Babylon's seventy years are up and not a day before, I'll show up and take care of you as I promised and bring you back home. I know what I'm doing. **I have it all planned out—plans to take care of you, not abandon you, plans to give you the future you hope for.'"**

— Jeremiah 29: 10-11 (MSG)

DAY 13

A Day to Reflect on Humanity and Worth

<u>Worth</u>

Despite a person's unfavorable behavior, they do serve a purpose. Even though they may not be operating in a positive light, we can remember who they belong to. Everyone is here for a reason and comes with worth. Yes, even those that harm us. Yes, and even you. We are children of the King. He made us in His own image. He knew us well before we were conceived. God has a plan for each and every one of us as we move along our own life's journey. We each have a purpose. When we consider this, how can we let a person, group of people, a boss, an evaluation, a slight, or a few offenses define us? We are God's special design! How can we also look at the antagonist as the ultimate monster? Remember, "we wrestle not against flesh and blood, but principalities, against powers, against the rulers of the darkness of this work, against spiritual wickedness in high places" -Ephesians 6: 12 (KJV). We must focus less on the antagonist, and use our authority and power which is in Christ Jesus to rise higher.

Day 13 Prompt: Reflect on this notion of worth. Do you see worth in the person that has caused harm? Is it fair to reduce their entire existence down to one act? Or a series of acts? Are they worth more than this?

"Overlook an offense and bond a friendship;
fasten on to a slight and—good-bye, friend!"

— Proverbs 17: 9 (MSG)

DAY 14

A Day to Reflect on the Sacredness of Life

Life Is Fleeting

The fragility of life is something many of us don't think about often enough. Life is so precious and can change in the blink of an eye. Ask anyone who has suddenly lost a loved one, witnessed a child's birth, or recently engaged with a new born baby. We don't know what tomorrow brings. We must not let the sun go down on our anger, dwelling on the past, and refusing to forgive. We must take the initiative to make the situation right. We must follow the prompting of the Holy Spirit to know when and how to make the situation better. Some of us are still angry at people that are no longer alive. We have to bring closure to that pain or we stop enjoying the gift of life. Accept what has taken place. See the blessings in the circumstance. Move forward honoring the miracle of life and not wasting another day holding on to or heightening the meaning of past offenses. God always turns what the enemy meant for harm into something good.

Day 14 Prompt: When you consider the sacredness of life—perhaps with reference to someone that you wish were still here—is forgiveness something you will prioritize?

_____

_____

_____

_____

_____

_____

_____

_____

_____

_____

_____

_____

_____

_____

_____

_____

_____

_____

_____

_____

"Now that you've cleaned up your lives by following the truth, **love one another as if your lives depended on it.** Your new life is not like your old life. Your old birth came from mortal sperm; your new birth comes from God's living Word. Just think: a life conceived by God himself! That's why the prophet said,

The old life is a grass life,
    its beauty as short-lived as wildflowers;
Grass dries up, flowers droop,
    God's Word goes on and on forever.

This is the Word that conceived the new life in you."

— 1 Peter 1: 22-25 (MSG)

DAY 15

A Day to See Others through the Lens of their Best Self

See the Best

See the best in that person. We all have things that happened during our development that cause us to do certain things or be a certain way. We are all imperfect, yet have goodness within. Sometimes our hurt, pain, and flaws block the true expression of that goodness. What have been good moments with the antagonist? What were the moments you were most proud of the person or grateful for the person? If you were to give this person a compliment, what would it be? We are all on a journey. No one is without sin, even our loved ones. Has progress at least been made? We can only overcome evil with good. What good can you do to counter this evil? We must strive to get to a point where we can wish the antagonist well, even without receiving a formal apology or changed behavior. We must refrain from looking at our antagonist through the eyes of their past offenses, but look at them through the lens of their best self, the same way God sees us.

Day 15 Prompt: How can you reframe your perception of the person and see them as their best?

_____

_____

_____

_____

_____

_____

_____

_____

_____

_____

_____

_____

_____

_____

_____

_____

_____

_____

_____

_____

_____

_____

_____

_____

"David confirms this way of looking at it, saying that **the one who trusts God to do the putting-everything-right without insisting on having a say in it is one fortunate man:**

Fortunate those whose crimes are carted off,
whose sins are wiped clean from the slate.
Fortunate the person against
whom the Lord does not keep score.

Do you think for a minute that this blessing is only pronounced over those of us who keep our religious ways and are circumcised? Or do you think it possible that the blessing could be given to those who never even heard of our ways, who were never brought up in the disciplines of God? We all agree, don't we, that it was by embracing what God did for him that Abraham was declared fit before God?"

— Romans 4: 6-9 (MSG)

DAY 16

A Day to make Allowances for Accidents and Mistakes

Accidents and Mistakes

We all make mistakes and sometimes accidentally hurt the ones we love. No one is exempt from mistake making. Sometimes we say or do things and later realize what a mistake it was. Although unintentional, accidents and hurts can have lasting implications. Unless someone brings it to our attention, we may never even know we wounded another person or how deeply it impacted them. Sometimes during an overwhelming moment in life, we close our eyes for a moment and something damaging has already taken place. Even if we did not inflict the pain directly, we may be seen as the reason it was inflicted. It could be our own anxieties and lack of awareness. It could be our words and actions that are mistakenly a trigger for another person. It could re-activate a childhood wound they thought they had healed. Can you understand how someone's words or actions could be an accidental hurt? Look at that person's track record before the incident. Look for their sincere apology. Look for changed behavior.

Day 16 Prompt: Reflect on this notion of accidents and mistakes. Consider how you would want to be forgiven if you accidentally hurt someone.

_____

_____

_____

_____

_____

_____

_____

_____

_____

_____

_____

_____

_____

_____

_____

_____

_____

_____

_____

_____

"Now, regarding the one who started all this—the person in question who caused all this pain—I want you to know that I am not the one injured in this as much as, with a few exceptions, all of you. So I don't want to come down too hard. What the majority of you agreed to as punishment is punishment enough. **Now is the time to forgive this man and help him back on his feet. If all you do is pour on the guilt, you could very well drown him in it. My counsel now is to pour on the love.**"

— 2 Corinthians 2: 5-8 (MSG)

"Here's another old saying that deserves a second look: 'Eye for eye, tooth for tooth.' Is that going to get us anywhere? Here's what I propose: **'Don't hit back at all.' If someone strikes you, stand there and take it.** If someone drags you into court and sues for the shirt off your back, giftwrap your best coat and make a present of it. And if someone takes unfair advantage of you, use the occasion to practice the servant life. No more tit-for-tat stuff. Live generously."

— Matthew 5: 38-42 (MSG)

"This is the kind of life you've been invited into, the kind of life Christ lived. He suffered everything that came his way so you would know that it could be done, and also know how to do it, step-by-step.

He never did one thing wrong,
Not once said anything amiss.

They called him every name in the book and he said nothing back. He suffered in silence, content to let God set things right. He used his servant body to carry our sins to the Cross so we could be rid of sin, free to live the right way. His wounds became your healing. You were lost sheep with no idea who you were or where you were going. Now you're named and kept for good by the Shepherd of your souls."

— 1 Peter 2: 21-25 (MSG)

DAY 17

A Day to Release Feelings of
Vengeance and Retaliation

Pride, Justice, & Power

Forgiveness is returning to God the right to take care of justice. It is truly a test of faith: Does God see my pain? Will God handle this situation? By refusing to release our hope for revenge, we are telling God we don't trust him to take care of matters. God will fight your battles. When we are hurt, we do not need to retaliate. I must surrender my right to hurt you for betraying me. There are no paybacks that are needed. We can say, "Lord, we trust you!" Retribution can also be fleeting. Forgiveness and a renewal of the relationship are really what many of us are truly seeking. Are you also holding on to the pain and keeping the hard wall of distance intact due to your own pride? Are you trying to prove a point? When we pridefully hold on to unforgiveness, we are at risk of losing our anointing. God's grace and mercy cannot flow in our lives. We are also showing a lack of care for the sacrifice Jesus made on the cross. He died for our sins. We don't have to act as judge and jury, and continue to harp on the offenses. Humble yourself, release your pride, and let God take care of the matter. Sometimes when we withhold forgiveness, we feel we have all the power. Forgiveness is not weakness, it is the exact opposite: it takes tremendous strength. There were times in my life I thought I held the power when I held onto the grudge. The antagonist was in need of forgiveness and only I could give it. We might fear going back to being powerless if we forgive, but be the one to end the power games. We must recognize what we lose when we hold on to a grudge. We lose our peace of mind and ability to focus on things that are much more meaningful. Don't let other people's bad behavior change you as a person. By not forgiving, we are allowing others to control us. Our thoughts tend to be focused on them.

Day 17 Prompt: Reflect on this notion of pride, justice, and perceived power. Are you holding on to the offense with a prideful heart? Are you seeking revenge?

"**Work at getting along with each other and with God.** Otherwise you'll never get so much as a glimpse of God. Make sure no one gets left out of God's generosity. **Keep a sharp eye out for weeds of bitter discontent.** A thistle or two gone to seed can ruin a whole garden in no time. Watch out for the Esau syndrome: trading away God's lifelong gift in order to satisfy a short-term appetite. You well know how Esau later regretted that impulsive act and wanted God's blessing—but by then it was too late, tears or no tears."

— Hebrews 12: 14-17 (MSG)

DAY 18

A Day to Release Feelings of Bitterness

Bitterness

Having an unforgiving heart can lead to bitterness, and a heart that is bitter cannot love as it ought to love. It blocks us from being vulnerable in new relationships. Once bitterness takes root, it is hard to rid ourselves of it. It's as if we are in prison, drinking poison, or committing an act of violence against ourselves. When we don't forgive, we are only hurting ourselves. Maybe it is worth repeating: By not forgiving, the only person you are hurting is YOURSELF. It does not honor you. We are attached to this person as the toxic feelings penetrate our thoughts and influence our actions. Don't allow the sun to go down on your anger. Don't let your heart harden and block love from entering your life. Don't remain the victim. Anger may be warranted, but does not change what has already been done and might continue to take place. It's as if we are waiting around for someone to confirm, "Yes you were right. They were wrong." Unfortunately, you may never receive that confirmation. Meanwhile, we literally hand over our emotional stability to the antagonist. Move on in happiness and love. Remember: you came from a well-being source. The joy of the Lord is your strength. Be happy and joyous. You have no time or space for bitterness. It slows down the healing process. Rejoice in the Lord! Reconnect to joy, love, and happiness. Heaven awaits us for eternity. Reclaim your life. Do something good with your pain. Bless someone else. Don't allow someone else to block the blessings that are destined to come your way. Never let a person's actions change who you are as an amazing person.

Day 18 Prompt: Be honest with yourself: have you become bitter? How has anger taken root in your soul?

_____

_____

_____

_____

_____

_____

_____

_____

_____

_____

_____

_____

_____

_____

_____

_____

_____

_____

_____

_____

_____

_____

_____

_____

"**Don't pick on people, jump on their failures, criticize their faults—unless, of course, you want the same treatment. Don't condemn those who are down; that hardness can boomerang.** Be easy on people; you'll find life a lot easier. Give away your life; you'll find life given back, but not merely given back—given back with bonus and blessing. Giving, not getting, is the way. Generosity begets generosity."

— Luke 6: 37-38 (MSG)

DAY 19

A Day to Release Feelings of Judgment

Judgment

Are we passing judgment on the antagonist? Every time we find something "wrong" in a person, we are judging. All judgment is harmful. Sometimes the source of our lack of forgiveness is our judgment of others (or ourselves), and what they could be or how they could behave. Judgment is usually unwarranted and unwelcomed. People are often doing the very best that they can under their given circumstances. Unless we ourselves are perfect and free from sin, we cannot judge others. Our judgment of others is often a weakness in ourselves. When we feel the need to have an unfavorable opinion of others, we have to look within, and take the plank out of our own eye. Everything we judge has a tendency to come back to us. What goes around does tend to come right back around, so we have to be mindful of our thoughts, words, and actions. God knows everything, including our judgmental words and thoughts. People are who they are (acceptance). When we judge, we are acting as if we are God, who is the only one who can judge. We all have blind spots, weaknesses, and areas we can improve. We cannot pass judgment until we have walked a mile in the other person's shoes. Their behavior could be rooted in deep unresolved wounds. If we are strong in certain areas and the other person is weak, we might subconsciously judge them for their weakness. We would not want the same judgment for our weaknesses. Leave the judgment and vindication to God.

Day 19 Prompt: Reflect on this notion of judgment. Are you being judgmental? What are you not looking at within yourself as you spend your time focusing on the other person's lack?

_____

_____

_____

_____

_____

_____

_____

_____

_____

_____

_____

_____

_____

_____

_____

_____

_____

_____

_____

_____

_____

"But Jesus' priestly work far surpasses what these other priests do, since he's working from a far better plan. If the first plan—the old covenant—had worked out, a second wouldn't have been needed. But we know the first was found wanting, because God said,

'Heads up! The days are coming
    when I'll set up a new plan
    for dealing with Israel and Judah.
I'll throw out the old plan
    I set up with their ancestors
    when I led them by the hand out of Egypt.
They didn't keep their part of the bargain,
    so I looked away and let it go.
This new plan I'm making with Israel
    isn't going to be written on paper,
    isn't going to be chiseled in stone;
This time I'm writing out the plan in them,
    carving it on the lining of their hearts.
I'll be their God,
    they'll be my people.
They won't go to school to learn about me,
    or buy a book called God in Five Easy Lessons.
They'll all get to know me firsthand,
    the little and the big, the small and the great.
They'll get to know me by being kindly forgiven,
    with the slate of their sins forever wiped clean.'

By coming up with a new plan, a new covenant between God and his people, God put the old plan on the shelf. And there it stays, gathering dust."

— Hebrews 8: 6-13 (MSG)

DAY 20

A Day to Acknowledge the Approval of Sin vs. Forgiveness

Approval of Sin vs Forgiveness

Approval of sin and forgiveness are mutually exclusive. The person could have done serious wickedness and evil. That will never be ok. We will never know the entire story. The scripture says, "Trust in the Lord with all your heart and lean not on your own understanding" -Proverbs 3: 5 (NIV). We don't know the why. Part of God's plan might include something that hurts us. It is during these moments that we really get to know God for ourselves. Difficulties make us stronger. Trust God and the process. Forgiveness allows God to have the final say while we release the bondage of the offense and wish them well on their journey. It means walking in love despite their behavior. We are not saying what they did was permissible, but we are leaving the hurt and the anger behind. We can keep our high standards of moral conduct intact and at the same time forgive.

Day 20 Prompt: Reflect on this notion of approval of sin vs forgiveness. Can you accept this notion that you can both forgive and not approve of what was done?

"**God, slow to get angry and huge in loyal love,**
    forgiving iniquity and rebellion and sin;
Still, never just whitewashing sin.
    But extending the fallout of parents' sins
to children into the third,
    even the fourth generation."

— Numbers 14: 18 (MSG)

A Day to Consider the Possibility of Reconciliation

Reconciliation, Renewal, and Trust

Forgiveness doesn't automatically mean a reconciliation, which may take some time if it happens at all. Reconciliation is restoration of a friendly relationship and a resolution. It often means two people coming together, having a conversation, and talking about the hurt. It takes courage and vulnerability. Both parties must swallow their pride and be ready for anything. It is opening the opportunity for a renewal of the relationship. You can reconcile and hope for a renewal of the relationship, but still not fully trust immediately, and that is ok. Trust needs to be restored gradually, over time. It is earned through consistency. If someone's track record has been consistent, work towards trusting again. Sometimes we claim to have reconciled but continue a pattern of mistrust. Everyone knows when there is a relationship without trust. It is often very shallow in nature. You must ask, "God, is this a relationship I should reconcile? Or is this a relationship I should release?" When the reconciliation process takes too long, many times one or both parties lose motivation and become apathetic. If it's a significant relationship that you would like to preserve, aim to reconcile earlier rather than later, before apathy takes root. If you are both willing to change the rules of how you interact and treat one another, you can experience a renewal of the relationship. Your renewed relationship may be a much better relationship than you have ever experienced with that person.

Day 21 Prompt: Reflect on this notion of reconciliation. Are you and the antagonist in a place to take a step in this direction?

_____

_____

_____

_____

_____

_____

_____

_____

_____

_____

_____

_____

_____

_____

_____

_____

_____

_____

_____

_____

_____

_____

_____

_____

"Hatred starts fights,
  but **love pulls a quilt over the bickering.**"

— Proverbs 10: 12 (MSG)

DAY 22

A Day to Release Toxic Relationships

Relationship Release

You might forgive but still choose to love from a distance and release that person from a front row seat in your life. Not everyone deserves that privilege. We don't have to return to the same relationship or accept the same harmful behaviors from someone who has hurt us and continues to do so nonchalantly. It is often helpful for the antagonist to offer some form of an apology, which in turn will allow the wronged person to believe they are able to forgive. However, we often don't get the luxury of an "I'm sorry," or even a slight gesture that the person is apologetic. Sometimes, they may send us on the up-and-down psychological rollercoaster of offending one day and then doing something kind the next day. Despite their action or inaction, forgive anyway. If we determine we should release this person from our lives, it is helpful to allow the person to feel our forgiveness when we do engage with them. We could help to lift some of their shame and remorse and engage with them from a new forgiven perspective, even if we are not close to that person any longer. Release them and wish them well. Ask God for guidance.

Day 22 Prompt: Can you forgive and release? Can you forgive and love from a distance? Where are you on your forgiveness journey? Have you determined it is best to release this person?

_____

_____

_____

_____

_____

_____

_____

_____

_____

_____

_____

_____

_____

_____

_____

_____

_____

_____

_____

_____

_____

_____

"God makes everything come out right;
    he puts victims back on their feet.
He showed Moses how he went about his work,
    opened up his plans to all Israel.
God is sheer mercy and grace;
    not easily angered, he's rich in love.
He doesn't endlessly nag and scold,
    nor hold grudges forever.
He doesn't treat us as our sins deserve,
    nor pay us back in full for our wrongs.
As high as heaven is over the earth,
    so strong is his love to those who fear him.
And as far as sunrise is from sunset,
    he has separated us from our sins.
As parents feel for their children,
    God feels for those who fear him.
He knows us inside and out,
    keeps in mind that we're made of mud.
Men and women don't live very long;
    like wildflowers they spring up and blossom,
But a storm snuffs them out just as quickly,
    leaving nothing to show they were here.
God's love, though, is ever and always,
    eternally present to all who fear him,
Making everything right for them and their children
    as they follow his Covenant ways
    and remember to do whatever he said."

— Psalm 103: 10-18 (MSG)

DAY 23

A Day to take Personal Responsibility

Self-Forgiveness II: Own Up

Are we holding on to unforgiveness because we ourselves didn't do right? Have we checked out or numbed out as a cover up for doing the challenging work? "I'm sorry" is an underutilized phrase. This could greatly assist with your own healing, as well as that of those with whom you are in conflict. We injure ourselves mentally and emotionally when we intentionally inflict pain on others. If we are inflicting pain, is it therapy, a religious group, or simply checking in with self? What needs to be done? Where do you need to grow up and mature? Seeking forgiveness takes maturity and courage. Aim to do better. All we can do is try our best. Write a letter to those from whom you need forgiveness. Apologize for the wrongs you may have inflicted, knowingly or unknowingly.

Day 23 Prompt: Were you being selfish and not behaving as well as you could? What do you need to own up to and admit? Where have you fallen short? Do you need to acknowledge the harm you have caused others, and the consequences that have resulted? Do you owe someone an apology and changed behavior? You have to take responsibility. What patterns of your behavior are you dissatisfied with? Have you committed to beginning a new chapter with an attempt not to repeat some of the same mistakes again?

_____

_____

_____

_____

_____

_____

_____

_____

_____

_____

_____

_____

_____

_____

_____

_____

_____

"**Summing it all up, friends, I'd say you'll do best by filling your minds and meditating on things true, noble, reputable, authentic, compelling, gracious**—the best, not the worst; the beautiful, not the ugly; things to praise, not things to curse. Put into practice what you learned from me, what you heard and saw and realized. Do that, and God, who makes everything work together, will work you into his most excellent harmonies."

— Philippians 4: 8-9 (MSG)

DAY 24

A Day to Shift your Emotions

Shifting from Negative Emotions

When we think about the past, rehash the offense, and consider the rejection, or betrayal, we might reignite the anger. Where do we put these negative feelings? We think, "How dare they have said that or done that? It was so unfair." Or "How could I have done that? How could I hurt my loved one in that way?" One day we can be fine and in a peaceful place, and then something reminds us of the past and we tailspin into the negative feelings again. Our hope and expectations were shattered. We feel duped. Lean into the hurt, the attack, and then let the moment pass by. It is only a distraction. It is only noise. Get back to God. Remaining in a state of anger will destroy you. Get back to prayer and gratitude. There are many ways to shift and you have to figure out the strategies that work for you: Refocus. Pivot to something that needs your attention, listen to upbeat music, pray, watch a comedy, or something else that lifts your spirits. It is important to feel good right now and for there to be no form of resistance present within us, in the form of anger, a grudge, worry, or any other negative emotion. We will never do our best and most creative work when harboring unforgiveness. We have to try our best to control our thoughts and be mindful of our emotions and how we actually feel. Seeing a situation as either misery or as a good thing is fundamentally a matter of choice. Staying stuck in negative emotions does not get us any closer to the peace and freedom of forgiveness.

Day 24 Prompt: What are we focused on? What goodness are we allowing or not allowing into our lives based on how we are looking at a situation? Each day is a brand-new day. Let yesterday's worries stay in yesterday. Try to approach each day and each moment with a sense of gratitude, joy, and expectancy. What are your methods for shifting your anger?

_____

_____

_____

_____

_____

_____

_____

_____

_____

_____

_____

_____

_____

_____

_____

_____

_____

_____

_____

"This is how we know we're living steadily and deeply in him, and he in us: He's given us life from his life, from his very own Spirit. Also, we've seen for ourselves and continue to state openly that the Father sent his Son as Savior of the world. Everyone who confesses that Jesus is God's Son participates continuously in an intimate relationship with God. We know it so well, we've embraced it heart and soul, **this love that comes from God**."

— 1 John 4: 13-16 (MSG)

DAY 25

A Day to Love

LOVE and Vulnerability

We choose how we respond in any situation. How can we respond with more love? When you think about the love you have for your parent, spouse, child, or a pet, we are at least familiar with the notion of unconditional love. No matter what they say or do, we still love them. Ask God to soften your heart towards the antagonist. We may never have unconditional love toward the antagonist but we can always aim to be more loving. It means we are showing God's love despite others' shortcomings and past missteps. We are tearing down the walls of separation that divide us. We are giving of our time, energy, resources, or something as simple as a smile. Love covers a multitude of sins. Love pays dividends. Not many people have the privilege of loving us in this lifetime. Forgive and love the people God has sent into your life. Try to recall good moments. Forgiveness in and of itself is love. Hope and endure for better days ahead.

Day 25 Prompt: Can you get to a place where you can truly wish the antagonist well? Can you see your antagonist through the eyes of a child? Are you strong enough to love and make yourself vulnerable again? Can you show friendliness toward the antagonist? Can you compromise and cooperate instead of compete and fight? Could you consider the possibility of loving the antagonist?

"All you saints! Sing your hearts out to God!
     Thank him to his face!
He gets angry once in a while, but across
     a lifetime **there is only love**.
The nights of crying your eyes out
     give way to days of laughter."

— Psalm 30: 4-5 (MSG)

DAY 26

A Day for Gratitude

Gratitude, Happiness, & Joy

Failing to forgive steals our joy. Decide to be happy. Visualize yourself fully forgiving others. Continue to shift from being indifferent, numb, or being dragged down by anger. Be present. There is a strong correlation between gratitude and joy. Keep a record of all the wonderful things that occur throughout the day, big and small. When you are grateful for your blessings, it is an easier path to becoming joyous. Take hold of your joy and happiness. How joyous are you and how much joy are you providing to others? That is the litmus test. Don't give away your joy by living with anger. Live with the hope that things will improve. Joy and happiness are choices. It's not based on people, things, or external circumstances—"I'll be happy when they apologize." Have peace and contentment in spite of it all. Find something to smile about despite what has happened and is happening around you. Where are the nuggets of goodness even in the midst of the storm? Be content with whatever state you are in. Take ownership of your joy and happiness by knowing Christ and imagining how much He loves you. As the attacks come, continue to abide in Him. Stay connected to Him. Remain with him at every moment throughout your day. He will give us His joy to radiate into this world. Reflect on God's word. Pray. Smile. Open your heart. Be forward thinking. Have a deep knowing who you belong to and who is in control. Forgiveness is God's command. We must obey his word and remain joy-filled throughout the process.

Day 26 Prompt: Reflect on some of the most joyous moments you experienced within the past few years. Can you see how harboring unforgiveness is weighing you down and blocking the joy from your life?

_____

_____

_____

_____

_____

_____

_____

_____

_____

_____

_____

_____

_____

_____

_____

_____

_____

_____

_____

_____

"Be cheerful no matter what; pray all the time; thank God no matter what happens. This is the way God wants you who belong to Christ Jesus to live."

— 1 Thessalonians 5: 16-18 (MSG)

"I still have many things to tell you, but you can't handle them now. But when the Friend comes, the Spirit of the Truth, he will take you by the hand and guide you into all the truth there is. He won't draw attention to himself, but will make sense out of what is about to happen and, indeed, out of all that I have done and said. He will honor me; he will take from me and deliver it to you. Everything the Father has is also mine. That is why I've said, 'He takes from me and delivers to you.'"

— John 16: 12-15 (MSG)

DAY 27

A Day to Reflect on the Lessons Learned

Gratitude for the Lessons:

The hardest things in life tend to teach us the most. Life is about growth and transformation. Take a moment to shift from the antagonist and think about the message they are sending you. Everyone that comes into our lives serves as a teacher. Are you a much more compassionate and relatable person because of what you have been through? Forgiveness allows the anger to subside. It allows you to look at the antagonist from a new human perspective. It allows you to be more in tune with God's voice as it pertains to that relationship. It makes us focus more on our own happiness, rather than the other person. It allows us the opportunity to be more like Christ. We must thank our antagonists for forcing us on this continuous lifelong journey. We can use these lessons again and again. I've seen God reveal things to the other person as I worked on releasing my own feelings of anger. I've seen others shift as a result of my prayers and my personal focus on internal work. The biggest learning for me has been the importance of feeling good right now, and ridding myself of any resistance. I now determine beforehand whether I'm going to approach a person or situation with misery or joy. Difficulties can serve as stepping stones to greater opportunities and blessings. Show gratitude for all you have learned in the process—about yourself, about others, and about forgiveness. Anything is conquerable. Consider how courageous and inspirational you are for forgiving. It is truly one of the noblest acts. It is one of the highest expressions of growth and evolution. With God, you can endure anything. You can endure, forgive, and become wiser. See yourself as an overcomer! Sift through the noise and extract the wisdom from the ordeal.

Day 27 Prompt: What are the lessons from this situation? Did you experience an awakening? A new way of operating? Based on this experience, in what ways has it strengthened you? What is it about what they said or did that triggered an unhealed aspect of your identity? How can you continue to heal that aspect of yourself?

"Everything in the world is about to be wrapped up, so take nothing for granted. Stay wide-awake in prayer. **Most of all, love each other as if your life depended on it. Love makes up for practically anything.** Be quick to give a meal to the hungry, a bed to the homeless—cheerfully. Be generous with the different things God gave you, passing them around so all get in on it: if words, let it be God's words; if help, let it be God's hearty help. That way, God's bright presence will be evident in everything through Jesus, and he'll get all the credit as the One mighty in everything—encores to the end of time. Oh, yes!"

— 1 Peter 4: 7-11 (MSG)

DAY 28

A Day to be Patient with Yourself

Forgiveness as a Continuous Process

Forgiveness is a continuous process. You might not be ready at this moment to forgive. Hurts might be retriggered too frequently right now. At one point I thought I had made huge strides on my forgiveness journey, but then I was hit with a family tragedy, and the antagonist's past behavior resurfaced again. I found myself tail spinning back to square one due to external factors out of my control. I was angry all over again. I said to myself, "They do not deserve my forgiveness." I did not want to bless them with that allowance. I took some private time to reflect. I am human and forgiveness doesn't happen overnight and in one shot. It is continuous. However, while I may not feel they deserve my forgiveness, I deserve the freedom and liberation that comes with forgiveness. It may take weeks, months, or decades to fully heal. We may have to practice forgiveness every single day. Uneasy feelings might resurface, and may do so indefinitely. We can hope the antagonist has changed and might finally show signs of improvement, but when they remind us of the past, we may feel a deep sense of disappointment. My decision to forgive cannot be dependent on another person's actions or change in behavior. It's NOT easy. There is something to the saying, "Fake it till you make it." Although forgiveness may seem unnatural at first, keep trying. This is not to say that you should live in a state of delusion, pretending the painful events did not take place, but we should make every effort to move past the pain.

Wounds will reopen at times, but live with the hope that the anger will subside once again. The faster and better you become an expert forgiver, the richer your quality of life will be.

Something else to note is that our unforgiveness impacts not only us but also our loved ones and those we must interact with daily. Everyone in your life suffers when you do not forgive and heal. Don't allow Satan to discourage you from continuing this process. HEAL, or you might transfer that pain to others. Our own healing is connected to our forgiveness. Be proud of yourself for any improvement on the forgiveness continuum you make. Savor each moment. The joy is really in the journey.

Day 28 Prompt: Reflect on this notion of forgiveness as a continuous process. Do you see this period of growth and introspection as a journey?

_____

_____

_____

_____

_____

_____

_____

_____

_____

_____

_____

_____

_____

_____

_____

_____

_____

_____

_____

_____

_____

_____

_____

"**Trust God from the bottom of your heart;**
　　don't try to figure out everything on your own.
Listen for God's voice in everything you do, everywhere you go;
　　he's the one who will keep you on track.
Don't assume that you know it all.
　　Run to God! Run from evil!
Your body will glow with health,
　　your very bones will vibrate with life!
Honor God with everything you own;
　　give him the first and the best.
Your barns will burst,
　　your wine vats will brim over.
But don't, dear friend, resent God's discipline;
　　don't sulk under his loving correction.
It's the child he loves that God corrects;
　　a father's delight is behind all this."

— Proverbs 3: 5-12 (MSG)

DAY 29

A Day to Trust God

Trusting God's plan

Try to develop an attitude of gratitude for where God leads us. We have to accept that we don't know God's divine master plan for life's events. We can spend the rest of our lives asking God why or pondering the "What ifs...." He owes us no explanations. In this life, there will be pain and suffering and no one is exempt; however, there is also an abundance of happiness and joy as well. Things are exactly as they should be. There are gifts that come with every life experience, even the challenging ones. If we trust Him, we wouldn't need to hold on to a lot of the pain that we hold on to. He is in control. He can turn any situation around for our good. Try to remove the attachment to the person and the pain. When you entered into this relationship, what was your original goal? Even though there have been diversions along the way, go back to that original intention. If we don't vow to forgive, the very fabric of our families and communities will unravel. Believe that this experience is strengthening you for something great. Only someone who has learned to totally forgive can handle what God will do through them on an even grander scale. At times, forgiveness can feel impossible, but choose not to be hurt and offended. Choose love over hate. Choose forgiveness over anger and resentment. Extend the olive branch, despite the walls and boundaries that have been erected. Life is a perfect gift just as it is, even with the difficulties. Trust God through it all.

Day 29 Prompt: Reflect on this notion of gratitude and trust. What are you grateful for as a result of this experience and journey? How has your faith and trust in God increased as a result? Consider the past. Has God ever failed you?

_____

_____

_____

_____

_____

_____

_____

_____

_____

_____

_____

_____

_____

_____

_____

_____

_____

_____

_____

_____

"But you, Israel, are my servant.
    You're Jacob, my first choice,
    descendants of my good friend Abraham.
I pulled you in from all over the world,
    called you in from every dark corner of the earth,
Telling you, 'You're my servant, serving on my side.
    I've picked you. I haven't dropped you.'
Don't panic. I'm with you.
    There's no need to fear for I'm your God.
I'll give you strength. I'll help you.
    I'll hold you steady, keep a firm grip on you."

— Isaiah 41: 8-10 (MSG)

DAY 30

A Day to Plan your Next Steps

Where Do I Go from Here?

What's next? Do you need to go through the 30 days again? Is it a plan to get closer to God? Is it a plan to pray for your enemies for the next 30 days? Is it reaching out to a therapist? It is often helpful to talk to a professional and get an opportunity to really articulate your pain. What else do you need for closure? Remember, each day is a new day filled with possibilities. God has worked on us intensely for the last 30 days and He will continue to work on your antagonist's heart as well. Enjoy the process. Trust the process. A good friend once said to me, "Sometimes people have disappointing moments, but those moments are not the entire relationship." It's true. One bad chapter in a novel is not the entire book. We are so much more than our missteps. Forgive everything. As was stated in the intro, the scripture says, **"For we wrestle not against flesh and blood, but against principalities, against powers, against the rulers of the darkness of this world, against spiritual wickedness in high places" -Ephesians 6: 12 (KJV).** Forgiveness is a weapon for spiritual warfare. The enemy is the principality operating within the antagonist. The enemy is beyond what the eyes can see and is working through another to cause various hurts, conflict, and disruptions. Extend grace, mercy, and forgiveness.

We are all living and learning through our mistakes that unfortunately hurt those around us. Continue to hope for brighter days ahead, free from the bondage of unforgiveness. You will soon walk in freedom as you forgive to live. Peace awaits you.

Day 30 Prompt: What's next? Do you need to go through the 30 days again? Is it a plan to get closer to God? Is it a plan to pray for your enemies for the next 30 days? Is it reaching out to a therapist? Map out your next steps.

"Enter his gates with thanksgiving
    and his courts with praise;
    give thanks to him and praise his name.
For the Lord is good and **his love endures forever**;
    his faithfulness continues through all generations."

— Psalm 100: 4-5 (NIV)

I thank you for your time, commitment, and courage to embark on this important journey. It is only when you forgive, that you can truly live! Despite it all, forgive anyway.

Printed in the United States
By Bookmasters